Tragic Theaters

by Natalie Lunis

Consultant: Paul F. Johnston, PhD
Washington, D.C.

BEARPORT
PUBLISHING

New York, New York

Credits

Cover and Title Page, © Katrina Brown/Shutterstock, © Alexandr Zadiraka/Shutterstock, and © Galushko Sergey/Shutterstock; 4–5, Kim Jones; 6L, © Bettmann/Corbis; 6R, © trekandshoot/Shutterstock; 7, © Mary Evans Picture Library/Alamy; 8B, © Eusebio Bilbao; 8TR, © Boston Herald-Traveler Photo Morgue, Boston Public Library; 9, © DIZ Muenchen GmbH, Sueddeutsche Zeitung Photo/Alamy; 10, © Photo by Ed Schipul; 11TR, © Hulton Archive via Getty Images; 11BL, © Bettmann/Corbis/AP Images; 12, © Richard Levine/Alamy; 13T, © www.doctormacro.com; 13B, © Picture History/Newscom; 14, © FCG/Shutterstock; 15T, © Album/Newscom; 15B, © AF archive/Alamy; 16, © Kevin Foy/Alamy; 17T, © Daily Mail/Rex/Alamy; 17B, © George Cruikshank; 18, © Ian Nichol; 19, © North Sydney Heritage Centre collection, Stanton Library; 20, © T. Charles Erickson; 21, © Bettmann/CORBIS; 22, © Photo by: M. Tungate – mtungate.com; 23T, © Chuck Pefley/Alamy; 23B, Courtesy of Albuquerque Journal; 24, © Dave Newman/Alamy; 25BR, © Pictorial Press Ltd/Alamy; 25BL, © Michael Ochs Archives/Corbis; 26, © Joel Maes; 27T, © Broadwater Productions Inc; 27B, © Montana Historical Society Research Center; 31, © iStockphoto/Thinkstock; 32, © iStockphoto/Thinkstock.

Publisher: Kenn Goin
Editorial Director: Adam Siegel
Creative Director: Spencer Brinker
Design: Dawn Beard Creative
Cover: Kim Jones
Photo Researcher: Picture Perfect Professionals, LLC

Library of Congress Cataloging-in-Publication Data

Lunis, Natalie.
  Tragic theaters / by Natalie Lunis ; consultant: Paul F. Johnston, PhD, Washington, D.C.
      pages cm. — (Scary places)
  Includes bibliographical references and index.
  ISBN-13: 978-1-61772-885-3 (library binding)
  ISBN-10: 1-61772-885-3 (library binding)
  1. Haunted theaters—Juvenile literature. 2. Haunted places—Juvenile literature. 3. Ghosts—Juvenile literature. I. Johnston, Paul F. II. Title.
  BF1477.5.L86 2014
  133.1'22—dc23
                                    2013013072

For more information, write to Bearport Publishing Company, Inc., 45 West 21st Street, Suite 3B, New York, New York 10010. Printed in the United States of America.

10 9 8 7 6 5 4 3 2 1

Contents

Tragic Theaters

Theaters are fun places to visit—most of the time. These grand-looking buildings are usually filled with entertaining comedies, dramatic **tragedies**, and exciting musicals. Yet what happens when the most dramatic and exciting events aren't happening on the stage? Many theaters have been the scenes of shocking murders, deadly accidents, and unsolved mysteries. As a result, they are said to be the homes of ghosts and **spirits**.

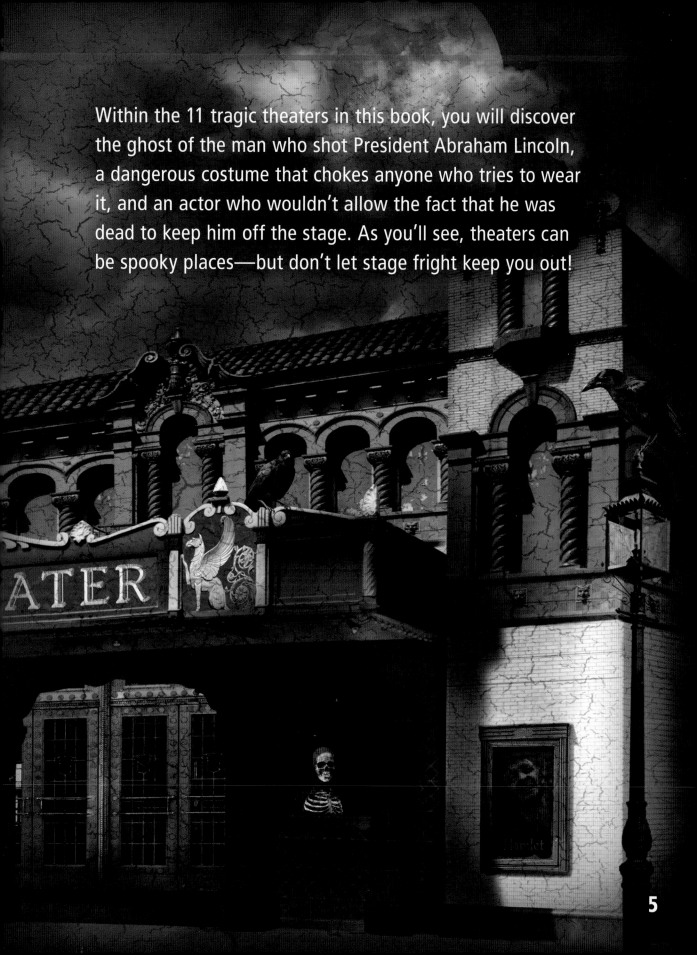

Within the 11 tragic theaters in this book, you will discover the ghost of the man who shot President Abraham Lincoln, a dangerous costume that chokes anyone who tries to wear it, and an actor who wouldn't allow the fact that he was dead to keep him off the stage. As you'll see, theaters can be spooky places—but don't let stage fright keep you out!

Lincoln's Murder Lives On

Ford's Theatre, Washington, D.C.

People expect to see a tragedy acted out on the stage of a theater. About 150 years ago, however, people in a theater in Washington, D.C., witnessed something truly terrible take place in the area where the audience sat. In fact, the event turned out to be one of the greatest tragedies in American history.

Ford's Theatre

On the night of April 14, 1865, President Abraham Lincoln was watching a play in Ford's Theatre. His wife, Mary, sat next to him. Around 10:15 p.m., a shot rang out. A man named John Wilkes Booth had just fired a gun at the president. A famous actor and a Southerner, Booth was acting in revenge. He blamed Lincoln for the defeat of the South in the **Civil War**.

Lincoln died the next morning, and Ford's Theatre remained closed for more than a hundred years. Since its reopening in 1968, some people have claimed to see a ghostly version of Lincoln's **assassination** acted out. Audience members say they have heard footsteps rushing to the area where Lincoln sat—followed by a gunshot and screams. Mary has been seen pointing at the stage, which Booth crossed as he made his escape. She cries out, "He has killed the president!" Onstage, Booth has sometimes been seen running away. At other times, actors have felt an icy chill—a sign that Booth's spirit may still lurk among the theater's shadows.

Today, part of Ford's Theatre is a museum. People who visit can see objects having to do with Lincoln's presidency and his assassination. Among them are the clothes Lincoln wore the night he was shot and the gun that John Wilkes Booth used.

An illustration of the assassination of Abraham Lincoln at Ford's Theatre

A Curse Strikes Again

The Longacre Theatre, New York, New York

The Boston Red Sox play baseball far away from New York's famous Broadway theaters. So how could a **curse** on Boston's baseball team also bring bad luck to one of these showplaces? The answer has to do with a business deal that took place about a hundred years ago.

In the early part of the 1900s, Harry Frazee was a successful businessman. He was involved in many deals, including the building of the Longacre Theatre in New York City.

The Longacre Theatre

Harry Frazee

At first, this large theater was home to a series of **hits**. Later, however, it struggled. Sometimes it stood empty, with no plays onstage and no people in the audience. At other times, plays were put on, but the **flops** outnumbered the successes.

Is there an explanation for the theater's lack of success? Some people think so. They point out that in 1919, Harry Frazee—who also owned the Boston Red Sox—sold one of its star players, Babe Ruth, to the New York Yankees. Ruth, who was nicknamed "the Bambino," went on to become one of the greatest home-run hitters in the history of baseball. Shortly after he was sold to the Yankees, the Red Sox began a longtime losing streak. The cause of Boston's bad luck has been traced back to the sale of Ruth and is therefore often called "the curse of the Bambino." Because Harry Frazee also owned the Longacre Theatre, many people blame the theater's losing streak on the curse as well.

Babe Ruth

After losing Babe Ruth to the Yankees in 1919, the Red Sox did not win any World Series championships until 2004. The Yankees, on the other hand, have won more than 25 championships since adding Ruth.

Playing the Palace

The Palace Theatre, New York, New York

Shortly after the Palace Theatre opened in 1913, just about every person in show business dreamed about performing on its stage. Today, it seems that many who managed to make it there also found it hard to leave. They were so thrilled by their successes that they continue to appear there—even after death.

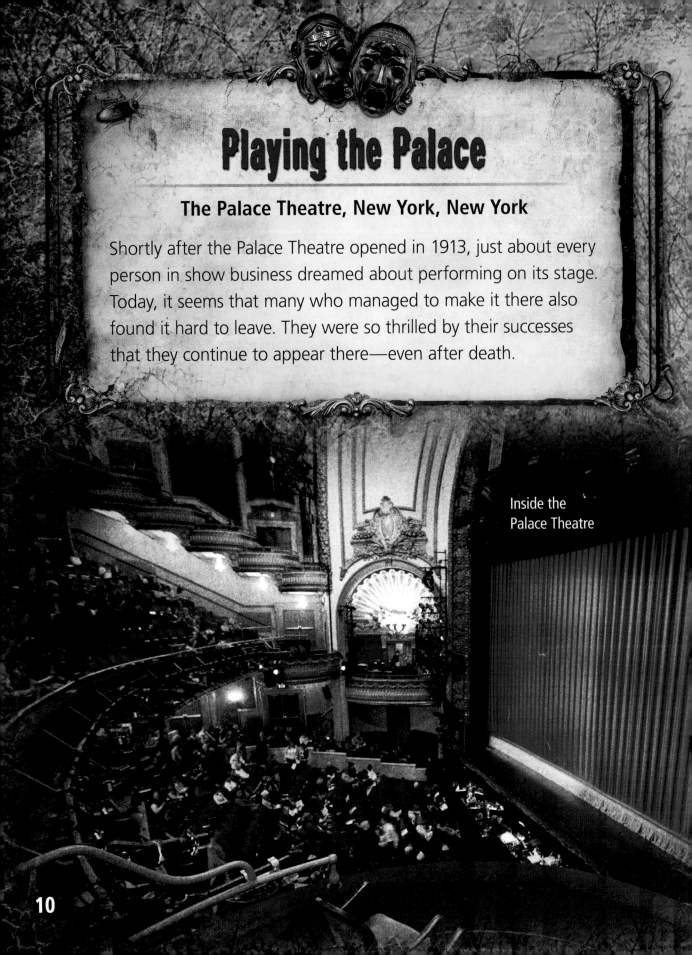

Inside the Palace Theatre

The Palace Theatre was world-famous during the time of **vaudeville**—a style of entertainment in which different acts, including singers, dancers, actors, and acrobats, appeared together in a single show. From the mid-1930s on, after the days of vaudeville, the Palace continued to be popular, presenting plays, concerts, and musicals. In fact, so many people have been onstage there over the years, it's not surprising that more than 100 spirits are said to haunt the building.

Some big-name performers can be seen in the Palace's ghostly lineup. For example, magician Harry Houdini has made his presence known to stage crews. Legendary singer Judy Garland has been seen near a door that was built especially for her entrance during her concerts. Other ghosts may not be known by name, yet they are still unforgettable. They include a woman in a white gown who plays the cello in the **orchestra pit**, a sad-looking little girl who sits in the balcony, and a little boy who rolls a toy truck on the floor behind a row of seats.

Harry Houdini

Judy Garland

Perhaps the most chilling ghost at the Palace is that of Louis Borsalino, an acrobat who fell 18 feet (5 m) while walking across a tightrope. It is said that anyone who sees his spirit will die within a year!

"Good Night, Olive!"

The New Amsterdam Theatre, New York, New York

In the 1990s, the New Amsterdam Theatre was being repaired after standing dark and empty for a few years. During this time, a night watchman at the theater saw a shocking sight. A beautiful woman in a green dress suddenly appeared—and then disappeared by walking through a brick wall. Who was this woman and why was she there?

The New Amsterdam Theatre

Lovely Olive Thomas moved from Pennsylvania to New York City in 1913, hoping for fame and fortune. She found both a few years later on the stage of the New Amsterdam Theatre. There she performed in the *Ziegfeld Follies*, a show that was known for its hit tunes and beautiful dancers.

Dancers in the
Ziegfeld Follies

Olive's glittering life came to an early end, however. One night in 1920, while she was on a trip to Paris with her new husband, Jack Pickford, she felt restless. Thinking that it would help her fall asleep, she took some powerful medication from a blue bottle that belonged to Jack. Tragically, the medicine killed her instead.

Shortly after her death, Olive began appearing once again at the New Amsterdam—this time, as a ghost. She is almost always seen wearing a beautiful green beaded dress from her days in the Follies. In her hand, she carries a blue bottle.

Showgirl
Olive Thomas

Because Olive is so well known to those who work at the New Amsterdam, the theater's owners have hung two pictures of her backstage. Each time actors pass them while leaving the theater, they make sure to say "Good night, Olive!"

The Phantom of the Opera

The Paris Opera, Paris, France

Built in the late 1800s, the Paris Opera is one of the most famous and beautiful theaters in the world. It is also the setting for one of the world's most famous horror stories—*The Phantom of the Opera*. Since the building where the story takes place really exists, could any of the shocking events in the tale be real as well?

The Paris Opera

Written in the early 1900s, *The Phantom of the Opera* tells a tragic and frightening tale. In it, a mysterious man named Erik lives in a hidden set of rooms under the magnificent Paris Opera. His face is horribly **disfigured**, so he wears a white mask to cover it. When Erik sees a beautiful young opera singer named Christine, he falls in love with her and tries to charm her by singing to her from a hiding place offstage. Later, he kidnaps Christine and takes her to his underground home, hoping she will grow to love him.

Erik from the 2004 film *The Phantom of the Opera*

The Phantom himself never existed. However, Gaston Leroux, the author of the novel, got the idea for one of its most thrilling scenes from an event that really took place at the Paris Opera in 1896. That year, a piece of equipment that helped the theater's huge chandelier stay balanced fell from the ceiling, killing someone below. In the novel, Erik causes a giant chandelier to fall onto the audience. It is during the confusion that follows that he snatches Christine from the stage.

The *Phantom of the Opera* was turned into a musical and opened on Broadway in 1988. It went on to become the longest running musical in Broadway history.

The Man in Gray

Drury Lane Theatre, London, England

People are often frightened when they see a ghost. Yet in one London theater, the actors and staff are happy to see a certain spirit known as "The Man in Gray." Why is his ghostly presence so welcome?

Drury Lane Theatre

No one at Drury Lane Theatre knows for certain who the Man in Gray was during his life. According to some, he was an actor who was in love with one of the theater's actresses and that his death occurred during a fight over her.

A number of important things are known about the mysterious man's ghost, however. For example, he wears a long gray coat, a ruffled shirt, knee-length pants, and a three-cornered hat. In other words, he wears the outfit of a gentleman from the 1700s or early 1800s. He never says anything, and he always appears during **rehearsals** in the afternoon hours. Most important of all, since he first began appearing in the 1930s, he has been seen only before shows that turned out to be hits. For that reason, people at Drury Lane are truly thrilled to see this well-dressed ghost.

The Man in Gray is not the only spirit who haunts Drury Lane. In fact, it is known as London's most haunted theater because so many spirits have been seen there. Among them is a famous clown named Joseph Grimaldi, who died in 1837.

An illustration of Joseph Grimaldi dressed as a clown

The Strangler Jacket

The Duke of York's Theatre, London, England

Places such as houses, theaters, and graveyards are often said to be haunted. Can an object, such as a piece of clothing, be haunted as well? A strange event that occurred at one London theater suggests that it can.

The Duke of York's Theatre

In 1949, Thora Hird was onstage performing in a play called *The Queen Came By*. She was a very good actress and was used to being in front of an audience, yet she felt strangely uncomfortable. It was as if the short, **embroidered** black jacket she was wearing as part of her costume was getting tighter and tighter—especially around her neck.

When other women who worked at the Duke of York's Theatre tried the jacket on, they had the same feeling. Reportedly, one woman even had red marks on her neck after wearing it.

What could have caused the strange tightening? According to some, years before Thora Hird's performance, the jacket was worn by an actress who had been murdered. Even more shocking was the way she died—she was strangled to death by a jealous boyfriend.

People say that after being used as a theatrical costume, the black jacket was bought by an American man who lived in California. His wife and daughter both felt as if they were being choked when they tried the jacket on.

On With the Show!

Oregon Shakespeare Festival, Ashland, Oregon

According to a famous show business saying, the show must go on. That's certainly true at an outdoor theater in Oregon. Here, one actor seems to feel that nothing should keep him off the stage—not even death.

The outdoor theater at the Oregon Shakespeare Festival

Today, Charles Laughton is best known as a movie actor. In 1933, he won an **Academy Award** for playing an English king in *The Private Life of Henry VIII*. In 1939, he starred as a frightening-looking bellringer in *The Hunchback of Notre Dame*.

Charles Laughton, however, began his acting career on stage in England and continued to appear in plays even after becoming famous in Hollywood. He especially loved acting in the works of **William Shakespeare**. As a result, he gladly accepted an offer to play the title role in *King Lear*—one of the playwright's greatest tragedies— at the Oregon Shakespeare Festival.

The role of the English king became more tragic and unforgettable than anyone could have imagined, however. Laughton died in December 1962, a few months before the play's scheduled opening. When the play did go on, with another actor playing Lear, people heard a strange moaning sound. It moved from the back of the audience and onto the stage. Next a cold wind blew toward the stage, knocking the actors' hats off. Had Charles Laughton made it to opening night after all?

Since its first appearance at the Oregon Shakespeare Festival, Laughton's ghost has been heard moaning many times and has sometimes even been seen. The ghost is said to be especially active when *King Lear* is being performed.

Charles Laughton in *The Private Life of Henry VIII*

The Boy in the Balcony

The KiMo Theatre, Albuquerque, New Mexico

Built in 1927, the KiMo Theatre is known for its beautiful and unusual design. Inside the theater, nine large **murals** show scenes from the American Southwest, while other artwork was created to remind audiences of the area's Native American culture. The stunning **décor** is not all the theater is famous for, however. It is also the place where the ghost of a boy chooses to spend his days—just as he did during his short but happy life.

The KiMo Theatre

When the KiMo opened, movies were becoming a popular form of entertainment. As a result, the theater's owners decided that it would be a place for people to see films as well as theater performances.

Inside the KiMo Theatre

By the beginning of the 1950s, movies were still a big attraction at the KiMo. Six-year-old Bobby Darnall gladly spent many hours watching them from the theater's beautiful balcony. One day, however, a horrible accident occurred. A boiler exploded, injuring seven people in the **lobby** and killing one. The person who was killed was Bobby Darnall—who had left his seat in the balcony to go downstairs.

In the years following his death, the little boy has been seen in the theater many times. He has also been known to play tricks, such as tripping actors onstage or causing lights to go out. For this reason, people working at the KiMo began leaving little gifts and treats, such as doughnuts, out for him. Their actions seem to be working. Bobby has become known as a slightly **mischievous** but mostly friendly ghost.

A newspaper headline about the explosion

The KiMo's name—which means "mountain lion"—is a blend of two words from the local **Tewa** language.

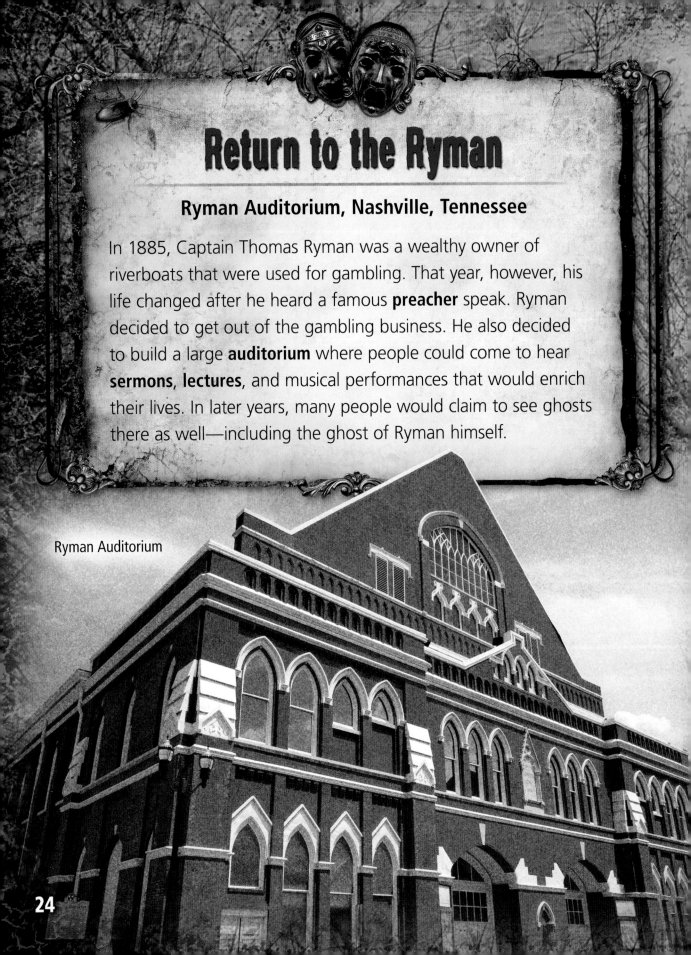

Return to the Ryman

Ryman Auditorium, Nashville, Tennessee

In 1885, Captain Thomas Ryman was a wealthy owner of riverboats that were used for gambling. That year, however, his life changed after he heard a famous **preacher** speak. Ryman decided to get out of the gambling business. He also decided to build a large **auditorium** where people could come to hear **sermons**, **lectures**, and musical performances that would enrich their lives. In later years, many people would claim to see ghosts there as well—including the ghost of Ryman himself.

Ryman Auditorium

For a while, the events presented at the auditorium that Ryman built were exactly the kind that he had in mind. Famous orchestras from Europe performed. Well-known people such as North Pole explorer Robert Peary, author Helen Keller, and First Lady Eleanor Roosevelt gave speeches about their lives and work.

In later years, however, the events at the auditorium often had more to do with entertainment than education. It was at this time that Ryman's spirit reportedly began to appear. According to witnesses, if a show that Ryman didn't like was going on, his ghost would make noise—so much noise that the audience would have trouble hearing the performers.

Reports of Captain Ryman's ghost started dropping off during the 1940s, when the auditorium became famous as a home for country-and-western music. Before long, however, people said they saw another ghost at the Ryman—the great singer and songwriter Hank Williams, who had died in 1953. It seems that even death could not keep him off the stage where he had given some of his best performances.

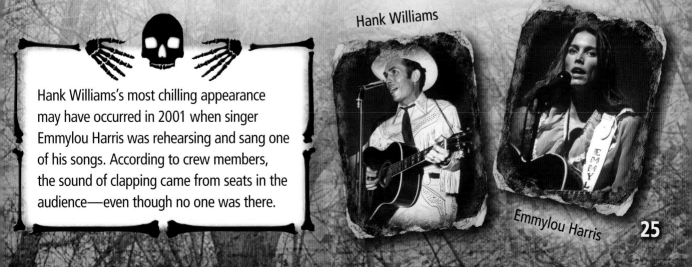

Hank Williams's most chilling appearance may have occurred in 2001 when singer Emmylou Harris was rehearsing and sang one of his songs. According to crew members, the sound of clapping came from seats in the audience—even though no one was there.

Hank Williams

Emmylou Harris

The Ghost in the Window

Grandstreet Theatre, Helena, Montana

The building that holds Grandstreet Theatre started out as a church in 1901. Clara Bicknell Hodgin, the wife of the church's minister, was beloved by the people of Helena, Montana. Tragically, she died of an illness in 1905. Yet many think that she is part of the community once again—in the form of a ghost.

Grandstreet Theatre

The people who built Grandstreet Theatre wanted their church to serve many different needs. So before long, club meetings, classes for children, and play rehearsals were held there. Clara Bicknell Hodgin led many of these activities. After her death, to show their gratitude for her wonderful work, members of the church had a stained-glass window made for the building. It showed a beautiful outdoor scene with hills, lakes, and a golden sunset. The window remained in place until 1933. At that time, the building was turned into a public library, and the window was put into storage. Then, in 1976, a theater company moved into the space.

The window that was made to honor Clara

Staff members found the window and placed it in the spot where it had been originally. As soon as they did, people started noticing strange things. There were footsteps in empty places. Lights turned on and off, and doors opened and closed by themselves. Most oddly of all, a special glow seemed to form where the stained-glass window hung. Was it a sign that Clara's shining spirit had returned?

Clara is remembered for the way she loved working with children at the church. Many people think that she now watches over the children who take part in activities at the theater.

Clara Bicknell Hodgin

27

Grandstreet Theatre
Helena, Montana
A spirit returns to watch over the building that she loved during her life.

The Longacre Theatre
New York, New York
A curse stretches from a Boston ballpark to a New York theater.

Oregon Shakespeare Festival
Ashland, Oregon
A famous actor makes a comeback—after his death.

The Palace Theatre
New York, New York
Dozens of ghosts still "play the Palace."

The KiMo Theatre
Albuquerque, New Mexico
A young boy can't bring himself to leave the beautiful theater where he died.

The New Amsterdam Theatre
New York, New York
A ghost relives her days as a beautiful showgirl.

Ryman Auditorium
Nashville, Tennessee
Two ghosts share the stage.

Ford's Theatre
Washington, D.C.
Do ghosts act out the assassination of President Abraham Lincoln?

NORTH AMERICA

SOUTH AMERICA

Pacific Ocean

Atlantic Ocean

Around the World

Drury Lane Theatre
London, England

A mysterious man in fancy clothes brings good luck to theater folk.

The Duke of York's Theatre
London, England

A cursed costume terrifies all who try to wear it.

The Paris Opera
Paris, France

A real theater sets the stage for a horror story.

Arctic Ocean

EUROPE

ASIA

AFRICA

Indian Ocean

AUSTRALIA

Southern Ocean

ANTARCTICA

Glossary

Academy Award (uh-KAD-uh-mee uh-WARD) an important award given every year to actors, directors, and others in the movie industry

assassination (uh-*sass*-i-NAY-shuhn) the killing of a famous or politically important person

auditorium (aw-di-TOR-ee-uhm) a building, or a large room in a building, where people gather for special events

Civil War (SIV-il WOR) the U.S. war between the southern states and the northern states, which lasted from 1861–1865

curse (KURSS) something that brings or causes evil or misfortune

décor (day-KOR) the way a place appears because of items that have been added to make it look interesting or pretty

disfigured (dis-FIG-yurd) changed or ruined by injury or some other cause

embroidered (em-BROY-durd) decorated with designs that have been sewn in

flops (FLOPS) theater productions that are failures

hits (HITS) theater productions that are successes

lectures (LEK-churz) talks that are given to share information

lobby (LOB-ee) a large room at the front of a building where people wait to enter the main part of the building

mischievous (MISS-chuh-vuhss) able to cause trouble, often through playful behavior

murals (MYUR-uhlz) paintings that cover walls

orchestra pit (OR-*kest*-ruh PIT) the area that is in front of and slightly below the stage and is where musicians sit

preacher (PREECH-ur) someone who speaks about religious topics and instructs people about how they should live

rehearsals (ri-HURSS-uhlz) practice times for performances

sermons (SUR-muhnz) talks that teach lessons about how people should live

spirits (SPIHR-its) supernatural beings, such as ghosts

Tewa (TEE-wuh) a Native American people who live in what is now New Mexico

tragedies (TRAJ-uh-deez) plays with unhappy endings

vaudeville (VAWD-vil) a style of entertainment that was popular in the United States from the 1880s to the early 1930s and featured a variety of acts in each show

William Shakespeare (WIL-yuhm SHAYK-speer) an English playwright who lived from 1564 to 1616 and is thought by most people to be the world's greatest playwright

Bibliography

Hauck, Dennis William. *Haunted Places: The National Directory.* New York: Penguin Books (2002).

Ogden, Tom. *Haunted Theaters: Playhouse Phantoms, Opera House Horrors, and Backstage Banshees.* Guilford, CT: Globe Pequot (2009).

Smith, Barbara. *Haunted Theaters.* Edmonton, Alberta: Ghost House Books (2002).

Read More

Lunis, Natalie. *Spooky Schools (Scary Places).* New York: Bearport (2013).

Parvis, Sarah. *Haunted Hotels (Scary Places).* New York: Bearport (2008).

Williams, Dinah. *Spooky Cemeteries (Scary Places).* New York: Bearport (2008).

Learn More Online

To learn more about tragic theaters, visit
www.bearportpublishing.com/ScaryPlaces

Index

About the Author

Natalie Lunis has written many nonfiction books for children. She lives in New York's lower Hudson River Valley—the home of the Headless Horseman.